KARL RAHNER

WORDS OF FAITH

Karl Rahner

WORDS OF FAITH

Edited by
Alice Scherer

Crossroad • New York

1987

The Crossroad Publishing Company
370 Lexington Avenue, New York, N.Y. 10017

Originally published as *Worte gläubiger Erfahrung*
© Verlag Herder, Freiburg im Breisgau 1985

Printed in the United States of America

Library of Congress Cataloging in Publication Data

Rahner, Karl, 1904–1984
    Words of faith

    Translation of: Worte gläubiger Erfahrung.
    1. Spiritual life—Catholic authors. 2. Faith.
I. Title.
BX2350.2.R34613   1987   248.4'82   86–29075
ISBN 0–8245–0788–6

CONTENTS

CONTENTS

INTRODUCTION

"The whole world was his audience," said Eberhard Jüngel in his obituary of Karl Rahner, whose views influenced important decisions while he was an adviser at the Second Vatican Council, and whose list of publications in many languages and editions spans more than four thousand titles. In his last interview Karl Rahner said about himself: "I have always done theology in order to proclaim, to preach the Gospel, to be of service."[1] The rich harvest of his thought and research, which he transmitted through his books and academic career, is bound to help theologians in the future fulfill their task among the people of God. In addition he wanted to serve people directly as a priest and as a member of a religious order.

It was possible for him to do this, first of all, because of his honest lifelong struggle for his own faith, and because he himself lived a hidden spiritual life, particularly of prayer.[2] It was

---

[1] *I Remember: An Autobiographical Interview with Meinold Krauss*, translated by Harvey D. Egan (New York: Crossroad, 1985).

[2] See his *Prayers for a Lifetime*, edited by Albert Raffelt (New York: Crossroad, 1984).

possible for him, because he never lost direct contact with people. Rather he came to know the questions, sorrows, and needs of individual Christians and communities through his own pastoral work as confessor, preacher, and retreat master. For many years he preached in university and seminary chapels as well as in ordinary parish churches; he spoke to both priests and nuns as well as to young people.

His own experience and personal encounters with others gave his words that authentic and genuine ring that touched people. His sermons and nonscholarly articles, like the ones he was asked to write on feastdays for the periodical *Stimmen der Zeit*, soon found an eager circle of readers, especially in small paperback editions. They numbered well over a million copies. With these, his "devotional" books, as he liked to call them, he was to reach beyond the theological community to ordinary Christians in their everyday lives. It was important to Rahner, as he tells us in the preface to one of these books, "that these small contributions to the theology of the spiritual life should help the reader to grow a little in that faith, hope, and love that is tested as Christian in everyday life."

But these texts also permit us a glimpse of Karl Rahner the man. One gets an inkling of the suffering he endured caused by many bitter misunderstandings and disappointments when he asks us to "let an injustice die." One also senses the realism of his spirituality, which he locates in the sober ordinariness of life: "Where the bitter, deceptive, and vanishing everyday world is withstood until the accepted end . . . there is God and his liberating grace. There is the mysticism of everyday life, the discovery of God in all things; there is the sober intoxication of the Spirit, of which the Fathers and the liturgy speak."[3]

His devotion also testifies to the bit of the child that sur-

---

[3]*The Spirit in the Church* (New York: Crossroad, 1979), pp. 21, 22.

vived in him, to his childlike trust and to the childlike goodness of his fidelity to the Church, to the Society of Jesus, to his friends, as well as to people in his care. He once expressed this attitude in an outline for a theology of the child: "The child is conscious that it has nothing of itself, that everything has to be received as a gift. It lives waiting for the unexpected, trusting the unpredictable; the child enables grownups to see that they can still play, that they can allow the true forces of life to transcend their planning and can accept those forces as ultimately good. That is the reason why a child is innocent and cheerful, with a Mozartean cheerfulness that is serene even when it cries, because it accepts even these tears of sadness just as they were sent, as tears of a sadness that is still profoundly serene. It sees a task accomplished when it is at the end of its strength, because nobody is given more than he or she can bear."

Behind his often repeated emphasis on the need to turn toward our neighbor in service, one suspects the diversity of Rahner's own mostly hidden service and help.

The memory of his own spiritual journey may have been a comfort when the shadow of death approached. The address he gave to the Catholic Academy of the Archdiocese of Freiburg on the occasion of his eightieth birthday might be interpreted as his spiritual testament. He implored theologians to stay mindful of the absolute mystery of God as the single decisive theme of theology. He also pointed to the necessity of humble restraint in theological knowledge in view of the fact that theology is in danger of divorcing itself from real life as well as from other areas of knowledge. In his concluding remarks he took the opportunity to appeal for funds for a particular missionary concern (to buy a motorcycle for a missionary in Africa), and in a quiet, almost fading voice he asked for prayers for himself.

"Attempts" is what Rahner called these texts; in reality they are treasures of spiritual instruction, especially for the everyday life of the ordinary Christian.

Out of the enormous number of his religious books we attempt to offer to a wider circle of readers a few central ideas on how to live the spiritual life. The first and fundamental idea is based on the sentence "You have seized me; I have not 'grasped' you." This suggests that we are more than we can surmise, that the great work of our life can only be "to accept ourselves," and that "whoever desires to love God already loves him."

The second characteristic feature of his spirituality revolves around his love of everyday life and of the ordinary as the hiding place of the "hours of decision" as well as around the theme of patience with one's neighbor. A third perspective returns to the beginning, recognizing the dignity of prayer as the only appropriate human language to speak with God. This is followed by an interpretation of faith as "faith within the Church" and finally by a reflection on the essential act of "kneeling before the blessed cross."

This reflection is offered in grateful remembrance for over fifty years of friendship with Father Karl Rahner.

Robert Scherer

1

YOU HAVE SEIZED ME; I HAVE NOT "GRASPED" YOU

O infinite God, you are the first and last experience of my life. Yes, really you yourself, not just a concept of you, not just the name that we ourselves have given you! You have descended upon me in water and the Spirit, in my baptism. And then there was no question of my contriving or excogitating anything about you. Then my reason with its extravagant cleverness was still silent. Then, without asking me, you made yourself my poor heart's destiny. You have seized me; I have not "grasped" you. You have transformed my being right down to its very last roots and made me a sharer in your own being and life. You have given me yourself, not just a distant, fuzzy report of yourself in human words. And that's why I can never forget you, because you have become the very center of my being. Your word and your wisdom is in me, not because I comprehend you with my understanding, but because I have been recognized by you as your son and friend.

O, grow in me, enlighten me, shine forth ever stronger in me, eternal light.

May you alone enlighten me, you alone speak to me. May all that I know apart from you be nothing more than a chance traveling companion on the journey toward you.

Encounters with Silence, 30, 31, 32

We are baptized. God has touched us, not merely by ideas and theories, not merely in pious moods and feelings, but by his own personal, incarnate action, which he works in us in baptism through his ordained servant. This is our consolation and our conviction: that God has already freely and openly spoken to us and poured the Spirit of his life into our hearts from the first days of our life. This clear testimony on the part of God is more impressive than the ambiguous testimony of our own heart in its weariness, weakness, and bitter emptiness. God has spoken in baptism: "You are my child and the holy temple of my own Spirit." Compared with the divine word, of what value then is our everyday experience, the practical experience that makes us appear to be poor, God-forsaken and Spirit-forsaken creatures? Our faith is in God rather than in ourselves. We are baptized. And the delightful Spirit of God's life is in the depth of our being where we ourselves, perhaps, with our smattering of psychology, have not reached. There in those depths the Spirit speaks to the eternal God and says: "Abba, Father." There he addresses us: "Child, truly beloved child of everlasting life." We are baptized.

The Eternal Year, 108

God's call is a summons to what is most individual. He established the beginning in love and irrevocable fidelity to his own plan; he lays down grace as our real and comprehensive beginning. But this plan is, precisely, one that plans that we shall be free, shall have a history, involving what we ourselves do, what we dare and achieve, what we suffer and what is our own. God does not diminish us; he gives us to ourselves. He disposes our life as something of which we ourselves have the disposal. He does not create statues, but human beings who, from the beginning that only he can give, can make and mold themselves.

Mary Mother of the Lord, 50

Christianity is what the living God does in relation to us, what the living God of grace gives us, in forgiveness, redemption, justification, and the communication of his own glory. Since, however, what God gives is not, in the last resort, a created gift, but himself, Christianity is ultimately simply the eternal God himself, coming to a human being and influencing this person by his grace, so that the person freely opens his or her heart for the whole glorious infinite life of the triune God to enter the poor heart of this tiny creature. This one total ultimate can be considered from God's side and then it is God's love for us, by which he gives his own self to us. Or it can be viewed in human perspective, and it is our love for God (given us by God), by which we accept God's gift, which is God himself.

Mary Mother of the Lord, 35

When God speaks to us and calls us, and we do the work of faith throughout our lives, and if we really love God and our neighbor through this faith—do not merely feel an emotion but love them in actual deeds of sacrifice—and if we are steadfast in hope because we know that we are pilgrims and that ultimate reality still lies ahead, if we practice this self-sacrificing love, active faith, and unshakable hope—then we are genuine Christians. In the divine Spirit that is poured forth in our hearts, we shall then be able to endure joyfully the afflictions, the bitterness, the difficulties, the trials of our lives, of which Christians have not less but more than other people. For the Christian is a strange kind of person who simultaneously experiences tribulation and the joy of the Holy Spirit, which is deeper and more penetrating than any tribulation, joy that is strong and active and endures unto the end.

Biblical Homilies, 156

Human existence is the unanswerable question. Our fulfillment and happiness are the loving and worshiping acceptance of our inconceivability and unanswerability in the love of God's inconceivability, with which we can learn to "cope" only by the practice of love and not by theory or the desire to understand.

Many people think they know where they stand: in themselves, in their society, in their life, or in their mission. Of course we know a lot about all these things. And why shouldn't these insights be our food and escort on the road to the inconceivability of ourselves and of God? But we notice increasingly how all knowledge is really only the road to (known and accepted) inconceivability, that the proper essence of knowledge is love in which knowledge goes out of itself and and we let ourselves go willingly into inconceivability.

6

How simple Christianity is. It is the determination to surrender to the inconceivability of God in love; the fear that one does not do this, but instead draws a line at the comprehensible and so sins; the belief that Jesus managed to achieve this surrender and in doing so was definitively accepted by the one who enabled him to achieve it; the belief that in achieving this surrender in Jesus God has irrevocably promised himself to us as well.

Christian at the Crossroads, 18, 19

There is not, in theology and in faith, God and then everything else imaginable as well; there is only the incomprehensible triune adorable God. When mind and heart are raised to him confessing their belief, all else must fall silent and be passed over in silence. Then there remains nothing for us but to adore and praise that Godhead. For the life of faith and the endeavor of theology are of course one day to blossom into that one life whose entire content is the loving contemplation of God face to face, the eternal praise of his grace alone. And yet there is a theology of the human person, a confession of faith that says something about the human person, not in the margin of the profession of faith in the one eternal God, but comprised in it. How is this? Because God himself, in the life of the blessed Trinity, in his ineffable glory, in his eternal life, has taken us into this eternal life that is his.

Mary Mother of the Lord, 24–5

If we learn from this believing, hoping, loving stride across everything merely of this world that we are children of God, if we accept all the more willingly what falls to our lot, whether it be poverty or loneliness or the inability to change the world around us, then we are truly following Christ, then we are surrounded by God's grace and love, then God speaks to us with that power which can never leave us lonely and abandoned, and says: "You are my child, I have loved you with an everlasting love."

Biblical Homilies, 16

There is indeed something more in our souls than can be revealed by daily experience, by modern psychiatry or psychology, my mystical communion with nature, by the exaltation of art or of love—in short, by any attempts of the human mind to grasp infinity.

Deep in our own nature God dwells, and this is no mere metaphor for the reflection of the infinite things within us, but the expression of a literal truth. God, the Infinite, the Incomprehensible, has been pleased to create us in the image of his own infinity and to take up his abode in the souls of human beings. By realizing this truth, we escape being enslaved by the finite things in our nature that would delude us with the pretense of our own godless infinity, and we are lifted far above the only infinity that we can indeed claim—the infinity of our own weakness and limitations.

God is within us, as he has himself testified. We are "the temples of the Holy Spirit" and "the Spirit of God" dwells within us as our true infinity. This Spirit broods over us, filling us with the abundance of the plenitude of life, anointing us and sealing our hearts with a celestial seal. The earnest and first taste of life everlasting, he satisfies our insatiable craving for knowledge of what we are and what we mean.

Happiness through Prayer, 25–6

The ultimate, irrevocable judgment, which exposes everything and judges everything, is not ours to pass but God's. God judges; at the end of the day it is he who knows our hearts and not we; he searches out all that is hidden and brings it to light. That is something beyond us, even if we are meant to have a clear conscience and must often examine ourselves. Important as it is, however, this examination can take us only part of the way. There comes a point where we are the people least known to ourselves. In reality all we can do is flee to God and his mercy. Poor, helpless, frail creatures, we can only beg him to make the crooked straight, to bring low the mountains, to make the darkness light.

God stands by us, even if we cannot always be said to have stood by him. He loves us, even if we are sometimes strangely forgetful of him in our daily lives, even if our hearts seem to be more attached to many things than to him, the God of our hearts and our portion forever. He is the one who is faithful to us, good to us, close to us, merciful to us. He is our light. He has come and always longs to come to us more abundantly. We should be optimistic about God and his mercy, for we have no right to entertain a low view of God and his mercy. We do not judge ourselves. If instead we let him judge us, being patient with him and with ourselves, faithful to him, accepting the life that he himself accepted when he assumed our humanity, trusting in him, then his judgment when his day comes will be grace and peace from God our Savior.

Biblical Homilies, 115–6

Heart of Jesus Christ! It is a finite heart, and yet it is the heart of God. When it loves us and thus becomes the center of our hearts, every need, every distress, every misery of our hearts is taken from us. For his heart is God's heart, and yet it does not have the terrifying ambiguity of his infinity. Up from this heart and out from this heart human words have arisen, intimate words, words of the heart, words of God that have only one meaning, a meaning that gladdens and blesses. Our heart becomes calm and rests in this heart, in his heart. When it loves us, then we know that the love of such a heart is only love and nothing else. In him the enigmatic mystery of the world's heart which is God becomes the crimson mystery of all things, the mystery that God has loved the world in its destitution.

Only in this heart do we know who God wills to be for us. Only by it, the heart of Christ, is the riddle, into which all the wisdom of the world leads us, changed into the mystery of love that gladdens and blesses. In the heart of Christ our heart is all-knowing because it knows the one fact without which all knowledge is vanity and spiritual nuisance and without which all the practical experience of our heart causes only despair: in the heart of Christ our heart knows that it is one with the heart of God. It knows that it is one with the heart of God in which even the thief and the murderer find pardon, one with the heart in which our deepest, darkest nights are transformed into days, because he has endured the nights with us. It knows that it is one with the heart in which everything is transformed into the one love.

The Eternal Year, 127–8

O infinite God, you have come to me in a human word. For you, the Infinite, are the God of our Lord Jesus Christ. He has spoken to us in human language. For when he says that he loves us, and that in him you love us, this word comes from a human heart. If this human heart loves us, the heart of your Son, the heart which—may you be praised forever!—is finite like my own poor heart, then my heart is at peace. For it loves me, and I know that such a love is only love and nothing else. Jesus has really told me that he loves me, and his word has come from the depths of his human heart. And his heart is your heart, O God of our Lord Jesus Christ.

Grant, O infinite God, that I may ever cling fast to Jesus Christ, my Lord. Let his heart reveal to me how you are disposed toward me. I shall look upon his human heart, O God of our Lord Jesus Christ, and then I shall be sure that you love me.

Encounters with Silence, 16–7

2

OUR LIFE'S GREAT WORK: TO ACCEPT OURSELVES

This is our life's great work: to accept ourselves as the mysterious and gradually revealed gift of the eternal generosity of God. For everything that we are and have, even the painful and mysterious, is God's generous gift; we must not grumble at it but must accept it in the knowledge that when we do so God gives himself with his gift and so gives us everything that we could receive. To do this is the wisdom and the chief work of a Christian life. If we look into our own lives we will find that we have not always done it.

All of us, young and old alike, are really latecomers. And yet God is willing to give us everything if we will only accept it—ourselves and himself and life without end.

Biblical Homilies, 25

It is a favor when God calls a person into being; it is an act of grace, of love, of kindness, of unspeakable mercy. But is this all that obvious? Is our experience of ourselves, of our life, of our fortunes, of our reputation, so clearly such that we can praise and thank God for conferring a favor upon us?

And yet it is so. He has called us into existence, an existence that is everlasting. He has called us into his grace, and this grace is he himself and his own eternal life. This existence, when we might never have existed, this eternity, behind which lies empty nothingness, this life with God in his sight, which is given to the soul in grace and in glory, all this is a favor because it is the blessedness of God himself; and everything else in our lives, anything that may threaten this existence of ours, is transient and temporary, a test and a trial. What is given to us through human birth is a favor from God. Can we look on this life, with all its mystery, in this way and accept it day by day from the hands of God?

Let us summon all the strength and all the courage at our command and say with joy: It is a favor!

Biblical Homilies, 35–6

We are all the work that God the Father has begun in his grace through Christ Jesus in the Holy Spirit. He has begun the good work in us, we have not. But he has begun it through our freedom, and it is always questionable, as it were —it is always the one great all-embracing question, comprehending time and eternity—whether the work that has been begun will be brought to completion.

Paul says: I am sure that God, who has begun this work, will bring it to completion. And we too may say this, frail and helpless as we are, we whose Christianity is always running down and atrophying, we whom the stream of daily life is always threatening to swallow up, extinguishing whatever light and power, life and glory has begun to emerge in our Christianity. Instead of studying ourselves we ought to say: He who has begun this work, and it is not we who have begun it, not we in our weakness, even in our freedom—God, in the glorious power of his grace, will bring it to completion.

Biblical Homilies, 134, 135

Our beginning is hidden in God. It is decided. Only when we have arrived will we fully know what our origin is. For God is mystery as such, and what he posited when he established us in our beginning is still the mystery of his free will hidden in his revealed word. But without evacuating the mystery, we can say that there belongs to our beginning the earth that God has created, the ancestors whose history God ruled with wisdom and mercy, Jesus Christ, the Church and baptism, earth and eternity.

All is there, everything whatsoever that exists is silently concentrated in the wellspring of our own existence. With what is hard and what is easy, delicate and harsh, with what belongs to the abyss and what is heavenly—all is encompassed by God, his knowledge and his love. All has to be accepted. And we advance toward it all; we experience everything, one thing after another, until future and origin coincide. One thing about this beginning, however, has already been said to us by the word of God. The possibility of acceptance itself belongs to the might of the divinely posited beginning. And if we accept, we have accepted sheer love and happiness.

Everyday Faith, 167, 168

Have we the faith, the stout heart, the humble mind, the docility to God's good pleasure to see in the most contrasting fortunes of our lives a chance to bring forth fruit for eternity, to prove our love for God, to be patient and courageous, unassuming and devoted; or do we insist on having our own way in the service that we offer to God, are we prepared to find him only in the particular situation we have chosen? Before we know it, he has sent us a different situation; and we have not the magnanimity, the willing, loving, uninhibited prudence, to perceive God's call, his work for us, in the different situation, to accept it with a will, to get on with it, to be well content with God's good pleasure for us.

If the heart is really kept open and ready for God, anything that may happen to us in life can be accepted as a grace and a blessing. Of course this means having a heart that is well disposed and humble, that listens and obeys. But why not ask God for that gift?

Biblical Homilies, 60

W̲e should remember the Advent spirit that John the Baptist, as Jesus' forerunner, experienced before us: a willing acceptance of the small, seemingly mundane task that this particular moment puts before us; a humble readiness to do the one small thing even when we see the greater thing that is denied us; unenvying preparedness to acknowledge a greater excellence in others, even when we cannot bask in the reflected glory; hope that the unutterable will come to us too in our restriction and imprisonment, from which we can no longer break out; the assurance that all finite things, even death, can be inwardly fulfilled by the eternal God of love and light, if only they are accepted in hope, and that every setback in life can be a resurgence; the certainty rising from all the graves of disappointments that even the cry in the wilderness will be heard by someone, and that all that sowing of our tears will bring forth a harvest of joy, even if only in the storehouses of eternal life; readiness to undertake a further journey even when we had thought that at last we were home forever.

Meditations on Hope and Love, 19–20

L et us be patient and faithful. Let us wait and accept the incomprehensible from God's hand. Let us believe, even when God tells us truths through his Gospel and through his providential dispensation—that is, when he tells us what he wishes to tell us through what we do not understand. Let us faithfully keep what we do not understand in our own heart. One day the infinite light of beatitude will burst forth from it.

Biblical Homilies, 64

W e are always in danger of taking scandal at what happens to God, to his grace, to his Church, in ourselves, in history, in our surroundings, in everything we see. More, are we not tempted again and again to think that this cannot really be the seed of God, that it cannot be his word, his grace, his power, his design, his handwork, his Church, his sacrament, if the results it meets with are so meager, so wretched, so precarious, so continually rejected and destroyed by the world? Certainly Jesus tells us in the parable that it is not the seed of God that is at fault but the ground, the stony hearts—it is their fault that the life of God bears no fruit in dry and hardened hearts, in blind souls.

But, one might be tempted to answer, is all this not part of God's plan too? The stony hearts and the hard ground and the thorns and thistles of this world and the devil and the hard-trodden pathways of our time? Is all this not foreseen and willed by God? Or if he merely permits it, is he not still responsible for it?

Biblical Homilies, 42–4

Your entire life is always held in trust for you. Everything you ever did and suffered accumulates in you. You may have forgotten it, yet it is still there. It may seem like a faint dream when you recall what you once were, did, or thought. You are still all of that. All of it is probably (yes, hopefully) transformed, fitted into a better and more comprehensive context, and more and more integrated into the one great love and fidelity to your God that was present, remained, and grew through all that life dealt you. Everything has remained, nothing has simply disappeared, anything that happened can still, as long as we are pilgrims of finite freedom, be recovered and transformed into the one "act of the heart" you do today.

You do not have to worry about your past, neither because some good has slipped out of it into nothingness, nor because of some evil (if it is redeemed). Both are still there, yes splendidly there, in what is essential, that is, in your genuine personal reality.

Vom Glauben inmitten der Welt, 16
Translated by Renate Craine

If the bitterness of life spoke to us of beatitude, if the truth we think about spoke to us of God's eternal truth, if the mysteries and riddles of this life reminded us that God is the solution and the primal answer to all mysteries and riddles, if all trouble spoke to us of everlasting peace, all beauty of God's surpassing beauty that cannot fade, if all the love that we are given and give had God in it to keep it new and strong, then our good intention would grow out of our lives of its own accord. So we must learn to listen more attentively, and pray for a heart of flesh to perceive the mystery of God in all we do and say and think, in all we undergo, in all our loving; a heart that will say yes, will perfect, affirm, consolidate the inner movement of our life toward God, making it pure and complete, so that our daily life will be steeped in a good intention.

Biblical Homilies, 152–3

3

WHOEVER DESIRES TO LOVE GOD ALREADY LOVES HIM

The first commandment is love of God, love for him with all our heart, with all our soul, and with all our mind. Love demands our very heart, what is innermost and ultimate in us, ourselves. But we will give anything away rather than ourselves; everything can be measured and filled except the heart. And this has to give itself to God forever and without limit. Do we love God like that? Do we love him as someone who loves, who is near and faithful, who asks for our love by offering us his own heart and his own eternal love? Or is God for us only the name of a supreme world rule, thought of in an extremely impersonal way, which one respects, with which one may come into conflict, which one really only wishes to avoid by fulfilling the commandments? To fear God is almost easier than truly to love him. But precisely this love is an obligation laid on us.

Our heart is so inert and tired. It is worn out with everyday things. And God is so far away. So it seems to us, the spiritually blind and lame. Consequently our heart feels it cannot love. When love is reached to it, it remains dumb, unmoved, stubborn, and even "good will" seems incapable of commanding the heart to love. No, of ourselves we do not have the love of which the first commandment speaks. Only he who demands it of us can give it to us. And so we will at least seek this love from him. We will pray for this love. If the first commandment is love of God, the first of prayers is to ask for this love. We must pray for this love. For God himself must pour out this love in our hearts by his Holy Spirit. He must give the life, light, and strength of this love.

25

Humble alarm at our lovelessness in regard to God is the God-effected beginning of our love. Prayer for love of God, a prayer that protests against our heart's secret and unavowed aversion from God, is our beginning of love of God. God hears such a prayer. For he has promised it to us in his most truthful word. For our part we should believe him rather than our own heart. If it prays for love, it loves, even if the poor heart feels little more than sorrow at still having fulfilled so little the first of all commandments.

Everyday Faith, 101–3

Our own honest opinion of ourselves is that we love God only in a half-hearted way—that, indeed, our love is often no more than a resolution and intention to love him, far from that "with your whole heart and with your whole soul, with all your mind and with all your strength," which he himself demands of us.

Yet, of one thing we can be certain. The person who has honestly resolved to seek the love of God may be said already to possess that love in his or her heart. For that very resolution is a proof that the grace of God has descended into the depths of the person's heart to kindle there a longing for God's love. What we must do is set no obstacle to the growth of this love within us, so that it may pervade our whole being more and more. We must ask him who is the object of our love to give us the sweetly compelling power of his grace; to reach into the depths of our soul and set a spring of love there so that its waters may make fertile the dry and barren places of our lovelessness.

Let us therefore pray: "Make me love thee, my God. Neither in heaven nor on earth have I anything but thee, O God of my heart and my portion forever. Make me cling to thee. O beloved Lord, be thou the center of my heart: purify it that it may truly love thee. Thy holiness, thy beauty, thy goodness are my happiness. Stay with me when I am tempted to leave thee. Do not forsake me: make thy love grow in me, for that love is eternal, and without thee I am nothing. Through this love, I fervently hope to be united with thee in life everlasting."

Happiness through Prayer, 39–40, 43–4

W e must take sin seriously. We must repeatedly pray: Deliver me too from my hidden sins. Give me a clear mind and courage to testify against myself on behalf of your holiness, so that I may recognize I am a sinner, so that I may not deceive my own self about my own sins, with the falsehood of this world.

But everything in me after all cannot be so perverse and evil, recalcitrant to the grace of God, as it sometimes seems. A good deal in our virtues may only be appearance that hides evil, but a lot of what is apparently evil and imperfect on the surface may only be the appearance that hides what God's grace in fact has triumphantly accomplished in us. In this life of darkness, weakness, poverty, ignorance, weariness, and grief one can after all be a human being who loves God and is loved by him, a child of God, living the life of the Spirit, sustained, enveloped, and inescapably surrounded by the mercy of God. If we look to God and trust more to him and his testimony concerning his grace than to what God the judge says of us and our wretchedness—and we may do so!—then we may also believe that our life and our weakness are really already so moulded by grace that in the very depths of our being there dwells, not the evil spirit of darkness, but the radiant light of God; and we may trust that we too are on our way to God, and that our life is already such that it will end in blessedness.

Mary Mother of the Lord, 80–1

O ur soul might seem an abode of hate and lust and greed fit for a devil's habitation rather than for the temple of God. And yet, the depths of us are not pools of stagnant bitterness, but the waters of infinity springing up into eternal life. It is easy to stir up the slime; but it needs faith to see, behind and through all these dark forces, a much more powerful force—the power of the presence of the Holy Spirit. We can conquer the depths of our own nature, and thereby realize ourselves to the fullest, only by an adoring belief and acceptance of this Divine Presence. Thus we make ourselves *living* temples through conscious acceptance of the Divine in the depths of our being. Only through such acceptance do we open our hearts and our lives to the full power of the Holy Spirit.

All this does not occur if we ourselves do not invite the Holy Spirit to speak life-giving words in our souls. He speaks within us in answer to the words he hears from us; and when once we have heard his voice, the depths of our being are no longer a tangle of conflicting urges and shoreless immensities, but a window opening on real Infinity and a place alight with the fructifying presence of God.

Happiness through Prayer, 27

One can love Jesus, love him in himself, in true, genuine, immediate love. One can and must love Jesus with a love that transcends space and time, in virtue of the nature of love in general and by the power of the Holy Spirit of God. This immediate love for Jesus is not simply present from the start. It must grow and ripen. The tender interiority of this love, to which it need not be afraid to admit, is the fruit of patience, prayer, and an ever-renewed immersion in scripture. It is the gift of God's Spirit. We cannot commandeer it, we cannot seize it violently and without discretion. But we may always know that the very aspiration to such love is already its beginning, and that we have a promise of its fulfillment.

The Love of Jesus and the Love of Neighbor, 22, 23, 24

Let us also step forth on the adventurous journey of the heart to God! Let us run! Let us forget what lies behind us. The whole future lies open to us. Every possibility of life is still open, because we can still find God, still find more. Nothingness is over and done with for anyone who runs to meet God, the God whose smallest reality is greater than our boldest illusion, the God who is eternal youth and in whose country there dwells no resignation. We roam through the wilderness. Heart, despair not.

The star is there and it shines. The holy books tell where the Redeemer is to be found. Ardent restlessness urges us on. Speak to yourself! Doesn't the star stand still in the firmament of your heart? It is small? It is far away? But it is there! It is small only because you still have so far to go! It is far away only because your generosity is thought capable of an infinite journey. But the star is there! Even the yearning of our inner selves for freedom, for goodness, for bliss, even the regret that we are weak, sinful creatures—these, too, are stars. Why do you push clouds in front of the star—the clouds of bad temper, of disappointment, of bitterness, of refusal, clouds of sneering or of giving up—because your dreams and expectations have not been realized? Throw down your defenses! The star is shining! Whether or not you make it the lodestar of your journey, it stands in your sky, and even your defiance and your weakness do not extinguish it.

How shall I set out? The heart must bestir itself! The praying, yearning, shy but honest heart, the heart well-versed in good works sets out and journeys toward God. The heart that believes and does not become soured, the heart that considers the folly of goodness to be more sensible than the cunning of egoism, the heart that believes in God's goodness, the heart that will lovingly let its guilt be forgiven by God (this is harder to do than you may think) and that lets itself be convinced by God of its secret unbeliefs, that is not surprised at this but gives glory to God and confesses, such a heart has set out toward God on the adventurous journey of a royal heart.

The Eternal Year, 47–8

There may be cases in which a person who truly loves God prefers to remain silent, content with offering to God her sincere desire for that love of which her cold heart comes short. We may feel there is no need to declare our love to him who reads our hearts. Still, we must reassure ourselves of this love, and God in his love knows the weakness of our

30

heart. His divine love accepts from us even that love which is not worthy of him. He loves in us that diffidence which makes us distrust our love and our ability to love. It is perhaps part of our unredeemed pride that, although we know how God loves us, we remain silent in modesty and fear rather than speak like children. This pride implies fundamentally that our love could be worthy of him, and that he loves us truly only when our love is as it should be. Let us abandon this pride. Let us speak to him as children, confidently and earnestly: "My Father, I dare to tell thee that I love thee."

Happiness through Prayer, 82

Faith does not add to our life a new dimension of heavenly realities from outside, it does not surmount our mundane reality, still less does it abolish this life in its dull ordinariness, with its slight happiness and its many tears, with its successes and disappointments. It puts squarely before us only the deep roots of this life which we would otherwise overlook or shut out: faith proclaims the radical character of freedom, of responsibility, of love, hope, guilt, forgiveness, and the ultimate ground of their radicalness it calls God. It is God who has always established himself within this life as its ultimate depth.

But this divine rootedness is that of our life in the concrete: that is, of our relationship with our neighbor, of our miserable daily duties, of our capacity for forgiveness, of our acceptance of life's dark disappointments, of our resignation in the face of death.

Opportunities for Faith, 8

4

LOVE ORDINARY THINGS
AND ORDINARY LIFE

God is the Lord not only of the holy days of life. He has created not only sublime things: it is his holy will that the little things also should live and that he should be glorified in what appear to us the insignificant monotonies of our life. We are his servants not only in lofty cathedrals where his mysteries appear to us in overawing splendor and enrapturing beauty. We are his servants also in the field or the workshop, at the desk or at the washtub. All this is for the honor and glory of his name. Therefore in this everyday life we must bear in mind that we belong to him in every department of our lives. Through our whole life, his praise must rise up to heaven and everything must be done in his name.

Happiness through Prayer, 49–50

When St. Paul says: "Rejoice with those who rejoice, weep with those who weep. Live in harmony with one another. Contribute to the needs of the saints. Be patient in tribulation. Rejoice in your hope. Serve the Lord," what else is this but a picture of our daily life, our daily life well spent, to be sure, accepted with its joys and its tears, with the tribulation and distress of others, with the hospitality we extend, with the situations we would gladly escape, where we are expected to do plain little things and are tempted to dash out far beyond our depth.

In these plain verses St. Paul tells us: Love ordinary things and ordinary life. Let life carry you along, with its ups and downs, its people, its laughter and its tears—all the variety that God's providence means it to have. If we would only accept our gift and vocation, accept our ordinary life as God's charism, our burden would be eased and we should be happy in this world.

Biblical Homilies, 97–8

It is obvious that we cannot pray directly all the time. We cannot escape from daily routine, because it will go with us wherever we go. Everyday life is our life, and our everyday heart, our weary mind, and our meager love that abases all that is great will ever remain with us. Thus we have to keep to the highway of our everyday life, its cares and duties. Nor must this routine be purely of intention. God must be sought and found in the things of our world. By regarding our daily duties as something performed for the honor and glory of God, we can convert what was hitherto soul-killing monotony to a living worship of God in all our actions. Everyday life must become itself our prayer.

But it can become prayer only through unselfishness and love. If we are willing and understanding disciples, we cannot find a better means of growing in spirituality than through our everyday life. There are the long monotonous hours of work, for which often no recognition is given, the continuous and painful struggle that receives little reward, the weariness and the sacrifices of old age, disappointment and failure, adversity and misunderstanding. There are the many wishes denied to us, the many small humiliations, the almost inevitable opinionatedness of old age and the equally frequent inconsiderateness of youth. There are such things as physical discomfort, the inclemency of the elements, the friction of human contacts. Through these and a thousand other trials in which everyday life abounds, a person can learn to become calm and unselfish, if he or she only understands these taskmasters, mundane and yet providential.

Happiness through Prayer, 52–3

The whole of human life in personal knowledge and freedom, and thus too in its ordinariness, is the history of grace. However little we Christians can forego moments in our life of explicit prayer, of liturgical worship of God, of express praise and thanksgiving to God in the holy community of the Church, hours of questioning and answering when we decide before God on the direction which our life is to take, it is equally impossible to restrict to a particular area of our life our religious life, our faith, our relationship to God, or whatever we like to call it. Our lives are worldly and secular, involve "intramundane" tasks and goals, are interpersonal communication; but it is in these very things—provided only that a basic decision for God exists, sustained by God's grace—that the life of grace occurs, our religious existence is realized, our eternal life comes to be. All this in the midst of ordinary life, through it and not merely passing it by.

Opportunities for Faith, 109–10

A Christian knows that patient endurance of the diversity and conflicts of life on earth is, in the end, the only way that leads through the reality of death with Jesus, the Crucified One, into the blessed incomprehensibility of the true God. She knows that the true mystic must always be prepared to leave her high contemplation, the mystical silence, to give a poor man his bowl of soup. She knows that the high feast of union with the comprehensible mystery can ultimately be only the result of the grinding weeks and duties of everyday life.

Über die Geduld, 56
Translated by Renate Craine

It is of supreme importance that we should achieve this conquest of our everyday life, because otherwise we allow ourselves to be dragged down to its level. Nothing can free us so much as this conquest. If we succeed, the love thus engendered will suffuse all the things of this world with the infinity of God, through a holy desire to exalt all the humdrum activities of daily life into a hymn of praise to the glory of God. The cross of everyday life is the only means by which our selfishness can die, because in order to be utterly destroyed our selfishness must be ceaselessly crucified. This fruit of that cross will be a love born from the death of our selfishness. Thus, through love, fidelity, faith, preparedness, and surrender to God, our everyday actions are transformed into lived prayer.

Our life remains what it was, difficult, monotonous, and unspectacular. It must remain what it is, for only in this way can it serve the love of God. Only in this way will it redeem us from ourselves. Through the sanctification of everyday life our desires, our reluctances, our stubbornness, and our assertiveness must be purified. Bitterness must cease to taste bitter. Routine must lose its monotony. Disappointment must cease to be sterile. Everyday life must train us to kindness, patience, peacefulness, and understanding, to meekness and gentleness, to forbearance and endurance. In this way, everyday life becomes in itself prayer.

Happiness through Prayer, 54

We should keep begging God with all our strength: Give me the light and strength to see the time I have as you do, to recognize it—though it may be distressing or wearisome or bitter, may even be the hour to die or to endure a lingering death—as your hour and your gift, as the day of your salvation.

If we could begin every day in this spirit, could accept each hour from the hand of God (for that is where it comes from), if we did not complain, if we did not beat our heads against a stone wall, but said with **faith and humility, in the power of** the Spirit and the light of the Lord: Now is the day of the Lord, the hour of salvation, the moment that can produce my eternity—then should we not understand our lives better? Then would not our days, however empty of human consolation, be fuller, brighter, nobler, ampler, blessed with the secret blessedness that the Christian can know even in desolation, even on the cross? Let us say once more with St. Paul: "Behold, now is the right moment! Behold, now is the day of salvation!" O God, by your grace give us light and strength to recognize and endure the day and the moment that you keep giving us as your gift, your grace, and our appointed task, so that this time, the time of salvation, may produce your eternity.

Biblical Homilies, 127−8

39

We cannot assert that someone who is well behaved and devout, virtuous in ordinary life, is also already certain of surviving the great situations where it is a question of life or death. The grace of such endurance is a grace that no one can merit by good behavior in ordinary life. But ordinary life is indeed the way in which we must remain ready for the decisive situations; it can be the way in which God wants to give us the very grace—which we cannot demand—of surviving the great hours of our life. We must be faithful in little things in order to be permitted to hope that God in his grace will also send us faithfulness in great things.

Opportunities for Faith, 117

Give us the knowledge, enduring in everyday life, that if we seek and long for you—the Spirit of serenity, peace, and confidence—freedom and simple clarity is *your* Spirit, and every spirit of unrest and fear, of narrowness, and of leaden depression is at most our spirit or is that of the dark abyss.

Everyday Faith, 96

Only by our daily prayer can we create the prerequisite for the great moments of real prayer. Only when we make the effort, however hard it may be, to keep our heart open, our mind awake, and our attention alert, can we be in readiness to avail of these great and rare moments of grace. In those moments, God will suddenly meet us anew, and we shall receive an impetus that will inspire us for some time to come. We must not miss that impetus. We must always be prepared for it. In an hour of trial, of temptation, of ecstatic joy or crushing sorrow, in an hour of unspeakable loneliness or abysmal suffering, we may be called upon to give an answer that can be rendered only in prayer, an answer decisive for time and eternity.

Happiness through Prayer, 48

Perhaps the turning points of life come only in the form of commonplace things. I may overlook them: the slight patience that makes life slightly more tolerable for those around me; the omission of an excuse; genuine acceptance of there being good grounds for someone else's criticism of me (how hard this is when something is at stake that involves my self-esteem); to allow an injury done to me to die away in myself, without prolonging it by complaints, rancor, bitterness, and revenge; fidelity in prayer that is not rewarded with "consolations" or "religious experience"; the attempt to love those who get on my nerves and not merely to put up with them by swallowing one's rage out of calculated egotism; the tolerance that does not pay back another's intolerance in kind; the suppressed complaint and the self-praise omitted and many other things that would be really good only if one practices them constantly.

We only need seriously to try to do such commonplace, everyday things. Then they become terrible. They are almost deadly if they are not taken in careful homeopathic doses.

Where one is rewarded by nothing more, that is, by nothing specific, whether outside or within, then in truth God is present as that "nothing," and finite loss is infinite gain. And appreciation of the latter is exercised by that loss. One pays for it in life with oneself. God is not to be had for less.

Such mysticism of everyday life is grace. Wholly and entirely grace. But that of course does not mean that there is nothing to do but impiously to wait until God's grace compels one against one's will. It "compels" in fact by bestowing the good will, and the good will thus given by God, viewed from below, is the great and honest endeavor of the human being him or herself. And this has to be carried out properly, by learning to form a taste for eternity in time by practice in the mysticism of daily life.

Everyday Faith, 65, 66–7

Where a responsibility in freedom is still accepted and borne where it has no apparent offer of success and advantage,

—where we experience and accept our ultimate freedom that no earthly compulsions can take away from us,

—where the leap into the darkness of death is accepted as the beginning of everlasting promise,

—where the bitter, deceptive, and vanishing everyday world is withstood until the accepted end, and accepted out of a force whose ultimate source is still unknown to us but can be trapped by us,

—where one dares to pray into a silent darkness and knows that one is heard, although no answer seems to come back about which one might argue and rationalize,

—where one lets oneself go unconditionally and experiences this capitulation as true victory,

—where desperation is accepted and is still secretly accepted as trustworthy without cheap trust,

—where we entrust all this knowledge and all our questions to the silent and all-inclusive mystery that is loved more than all our individual knowledge that makes us such small people,

—where we rehearse our own deaths in everyday life, and try to live in such a way as we would like to die, peaceful and composed,

—where . . . (we could go on and on):

—there is God and his liberating grace. There we find what we Christians call the Holy Spirit of God. There is the mysticism of everyday life, the discovery of God in all things; there is the sober intoxication of the Spirit, of which the Fathers and the liturgy speak, which we cannot reject or despise, because it is real.

The Spirit in the Church, 21–2

When would a moment of my time be "fulfilled," as we speak of the "fullness" of time that came for the world as a whole with the incarnate Word of God? Evidently it would occur if a moment came in which, with complete awareness, courage, and determination, I had concentrated myself completely and, having collected myself entirely and comprised myself in my freedom, I gave myself wholly to God.

But when does such an act take place in me? When do I concentrate myself wholly and in entire freedom give myself to God? Somewhere or other in my life the moment of the fullness of time must nevertheless occur. That one, comprehensive, great and holy event must occur, the moment in which a person's heart gives him or her so wholly into the hands of the Incomprehensible that the gift is not secretly taken back again, as mostly happens.

Where is the fullness of time in my life, where is the decisive hour that comprises the whole of my human reality?

People often speak of the greatest hours, the finest and holiest moments of human life, and mean by them—according to what is being celebrated—first communion, wedding day, the reception of the Body of Christ, ordination, and so on. Are these events the turning points of life that we are seeking? Are they the fullness of eternity entering into a moment of time? We might think so. And yet everyone knows that with the fullness of the sacrament one does not always receive the fullness of what the sacrament signifies and of itself contains, the fullness of grace.

It is therefore possible that the greater hour, the time of greater plenitude, may occur where the sign (in the wider sense) is poorer and more ambiguous and not an *opus operatum*. It may be that one person will drain the chalice of his life with his life and his death in an hour which is not that of the eucharistic meal. It is possible that someone may suddenly break through all the barriers that previously fenced in his or her anxious egotism and emerge into the vastness of God, in a silent, unnoticed resignation, in an apparently small sacrifice.

Consequently it is possible that an onion or two thrown over the garden fence to a poor man may be a decisive turning point —a little kindness that really forgets to look for gratitude, forgiveness that does not notice at all that it is forgiving, silent endurance of mortal pain without bitterness. Such decisive hours do in fact exist. They can exist. But one does not have them merely by talking about them. And not every experience is an experience accepted and grasped with the utmost strength of heart. We have not the fullness of time and eternity contained in our heart simply because we have enjoyed a small taste of it and are philosophizing grandly about this small sample.

And so the question remains: Has such a decisive hour of the fullness of my time occurred? A foolish question. One cannot really ask it in that way. For, of course, it would be of no use to me if I could make such a statement about an earlier moment of my life. The earlier is always only the summons to bring about what has already been, and the promise that what has already succeeded will also succeed now.

Everyday Faith, 55, 56, 57, 58–9, 60, 61–2, 63, 64

5

BEARING IN PATIENCE
THE SOULS OF MY BRETHREN

We human beings are important for one another. We mean something to one another, not only in the everyday things of life. Even in our salvation we are also similarly dependent on other human beings.

Since we belong to one another, not only in everyday life, in politics and secular history, but in the unfolding course of history, there is, then, a history of grace and salvation, in which we all belong to one another, and so none is without importance for the others, and all are important for each individual. Each must bear the load of guilt and grace, not only for himself or herself, but also for all the rest. What one suffers, prays, weeps over, endures, and finds blessedness in is of decisive importance for everyone.

The community of humankind is a community of eternal welfare or loss, a vast community that acts out as a whole, and not only in individual human beings, the great drama of history before the eyes of God, and which brings to light what God's thoughts about humankind was.

Since, in Jesus Christ and in him alone, salvation has come to us, to the one community of the human race, in which all are interdependent, God in his grace and mercy has also decreed that one should help the other, even in the attainment and bestowing of salvation.

We are intermediaries and in this sense mediators of grace for each other, and so we shall be held to account before the judgment seat of God, whether, within the measure of our possibilities, in our situation in life, through the gifts and talents we were endowed with, we did for others what we ought to have done, as intermediaries on behalf of our neighbors.

To be sure we are always called singly, individually, one by one, by the grace of God, which is always intended precisely for the individual. Nevertheless, unique individuals as we are, we are loved by God not only because we belong to all others and because they belong to us. Because God loves them, he loves us, and because he loves us, he loves the others.

Mary Mother of the Lord, 26, 27, 28, 96–7, 98

When we look at the average Christian life, it would seem that the notion prevailing in the normal Christian's moral consciousness is that we have "loved our neighbor" when we have done nothing evil to him or her, and have met the objective claims he or she may justly have against us. The truth, however, is that we are commanded by the "commandment" to love our neighbor, in its oneness with the commandment to love God, is the demolition of our own selfishness— the overthrow of the notion that love of neighbor is basically really only the rational settlement of mutual claims, that it demands giving and taking only to the mutual satisfaction of all parties. In reality, Christian love of neighbor attains its true essence only where no more accounts are kept, where a readiness prevails to love without requital, where, in the love of neighbor as well, the folly of the cross is accepted and welcomed.

When one really understands the unity of the love of God and neighbor, the latter shifts from its position as a particular demand for a delimited, verifiable achievement to a position of total fulfillment of one's life, in which we are challenged in our

totality, wholly challenged, challenged beyond our capacity—
but challenged in the only way in which we may gain the
highest freedom: freedom from ourselves.

The Love of Jesus and the Love of Neighbor, 83–4

When we look into our own hearts, how difficult the
whole thing is: we cannot seem to get away from ourselves, we are always turning back to ourselves, we do not
seem able to give our hearts away. And sometimes when we
think that we have done it, is the truth not that we want the
other person to give herself to us but have no mind to give ourselves to her just as she is?

When love enters the picture, when we give ourselves with
all our divine infinity to our neighbor, then all calculations of
commutative justice and legality are superseded. Then we are
no longer accomplishing something or rendering a service; we
do more than comply with an objective norm that is equally
binding on us all; we are perfecting ourselves by being the
unique creatures we are meant to be, perfecting ourselves because God has given us his own divine self in a unique way.
And because what is involved here is a person, unique and irreplaceable, a person who achieves and perfects herself by lovingly giving herself away to others, all mere legality is supera-
bundantly fulfilled and left behind. Thus love is the fulfilling
of the law and the bond of perfection, as Paul says—that which
will not pass away.

Biblical Preaching, 105–7

Every one of us is a burden to our neighbor and perhaps for that very reason—alas, how slow we are to grasp the fact—a grace. Our neighbor may wrong us. He may really be a burden to us, and perhaps he should not be. And yet, even such burdens should be an extra weight of grace for a Christian. So we should bear them and forgive our neighbor any extra weight there may be through his fault.

The Greek term Paul uses to convey this forgiveness includes the word "*charis*," pardon. Accordingly he continues: "As the Lord has forgiven you, so you also must forgive." We must forgive one another, as the Lord has forgiven us. Or did he not have to forgive us? Did we not need his pardon, poor sinners that we were, whose sins, whose monstrous sins, our Lord God had to forgive us in Jesus Christ? Why then can we not do the same?

Biblical Homilies, 148–9

Somewhere, even in the most normal course of a middle-class life, there are moments in which that process calls a relative halt. It contains gaps and cracks that look like empty fissures but that, once we look hard, permit glimpses into the infinite. From time to time there seems to occur in every human life, no matter whose, moments in which the sober everyday love that can scarcely be distinguished from reasonable selfishness suddenly finds itself confronted by the invitation to love without hope of requital, to trust without looking back, to dare to love where only a foolish adventure can reasonably be expected, one that "would never be worth it."

At such moments, human beings' freedom finds itself standing before the choice either of being cautiously cowardly, denying itself and not daring to risk itself, or, in a foolhardy trustfulness (seemingly absurd and yet—wonder of wonders—there it is), of taking the risk, of risking our freedom without looking back, of risking really loving in the proper sense of the word. There is no longer any ground to tap in advance to see if it is solid or not; then freedom dares more than is granted it by a calculating rationality, risks itself and its own subject, and plunges into the unfathomable, unbounded dwelling place of God, who can ultimately be experienced only in this bottomless, headlong plunge. To be sure, this blind leap is ultimately occasioned, made possible, and snatched up by what we call God's grace, which alone grants the freedom to take such an unconditional leap. But this in no way militates against the fact that a like miracle of infinite freedom and love, and hence of a communion of brothers and sisters, can occur in the midst of the banality of everyday life. The launching pad, if we may so call it, may be flimsy and narrow and rise so scarcely above the flat plain of the everyday as to be hardly noticed at all. But these trivialities—the biblical glass of water to someone thirsty, a kind word at someone's sickbed, the refusal to take some small, mean advantage even of someone whose selfishness has infuriated us, or a thousand other everyday trifles—can be the unassuming accomplishment by which the actual attitude of unselfish brotherly and sisterly communion is consummated. And this communion is life's proper deed.

Christian faith is of the conviction that only love for God and human beings, which is more than a commandment and obligatory exercise, brings human beings to salvation. It has the conviction that this love is the meaning of the whole of the Law and the prophets, but that it can occur even in the humble, ordinary everyday—and that it is just there, in the everyday, unobtrusively, that the last renunciation and the last surrender to God can occur that admits us to a participation in the final deed of Jesus on the cross. A love of neighbor as one's brother and sister, a communion of brothers and sisters having a love of God both as its vehicle and as its consummation, is the highest thing of all. And this highest thing of all is a possibility, an opportunity, offered to every human being.

The Love of Jesus and the Love of Neighbor, 102–4

Have I ever, ever once, loved in such a manner that no echo, no reward, no recognition, no self-attestation or endorsement answered this love? Have I even once in my life loved with the terrible feeling that I was nothing but stupid, simply made a fool of and used? These experiences, these tests of unselfish love, to be sure, leave something to be desired with respect to a cheery, blissful experience.

But wherever a human being, in his or her love, is unable to bear its bitter disappointments mutely and without question, he or she must still wonder: Have I not confused a worldly-wise selfishness that can behave very respectably with true love that makes a human being really selfless and releases him or her to sink away into the incomprehensibility of God?

The Love of Jesus and the Love of Neighbor, 84

Could we not say to God: Here is the person I cannot manage to get on with. He belongs to you. You made him. If you do not will him to be the way he is, at least you allow him to be that way. Dear God, I want to put up with him the way you put up with me.

Biblical Homilies, 178

Haven't I enough burdens of my own to bear? Isn't my heart weak and miserable enough with its own troubles, without adding to it the crushing woes of others?

Do I regain my own inner strength precisely by being steadfast and courageous in the service of my brethren, and thereby giving testimony to the world that your heart is bigger than ours, that you are patient and long suffering, that your mercy never disdains us, that your love is never outdone by our wretchedness? Is that the best way to take care of myself, by forgetting myself in the care of others?

If your sending me out was an act of your mercy to me, O Lord—and how can I doubt that it was?—then it must be so. Then you must desire that I possess my own soul in patience, precisely through bearing in patience the souls of my brethren.

Encounters with Silence, 64

Only in a communion of brothers and sisters is the human being genuinely encountered as a human being. The human being is ultimately a—no, *the* mystery, conditioned by and grounded in the mystery of God.

The love of neighbor will make the loving person over to the other, surrender him or her to the other, not simply in this or that surveillable and manipulable particularity (of utility, objective advantage, comfort in one's vital needs, esthetic infatuation, and so on), but as a whole—as "subject," as a person with an unsurveillable, limitless breadth of unbounded consciousness and concrete freedom, as a person who surrenders and loses himself or herself in abandonment to God. And vice versa: The beloved accepts the other in this love of neighbor, accepts the other as this incalculably mysterious subject. Love of neighbor is the compenetration of two such mysteries, in which mystery—God—is present absolutely.

The Love of Jesus and the Love of Neighbor, 99, 100

6

RECOGNIZE THE WORTH
OF YOUR PRAYER

Since we are partakers in the divine nature, our prayer has a greater power than lies in mere human words. We pray not only with what is human in us but also with what is divine. Mighty things, far beyond our understanding, occur within us when we say: "Our Father." They may seem to us to be dryly spoken and to savor of presumption; but when sincerely spoken, the inner reality to which they correspond is something glorious. We are baptized children of God, professing our belief in him and our love for him; therefore the Spirit of God truly lives within us and speaks in us. Through the Holy Spirit dwelling within us, the words "Our Father" are filled with a power of worship that links them with the praise of God by the angelic choirs in heaven.

Happiness through Prayer, 28

It is only by grace that we can learn how to pray, but our willingness to pray and our perseverance in praying play an important part. We must learn to concentrate, in interior silence, on what we are about to do, namely to lift up our hearts. We must learn to speak to God without using set words; we must speak to him of our necessities, of our daily life, in particular of that secret resistance against speaking to him about our duties. We must speak to him of our loved ones, of our moods, of the world and its needs, of the dead who have gone before us, and of himself. Our words must tell of his greatness and distance, incomprehensible and yet wonderful, of his truth in contrast to our untruth, of his love and our selfishness. He is Life, while we are death; he is fulfillment, while we are but longing. We must also learn to mute those things that keep us anxious and tensed if we wish to attain to real interior quietude.

We must learn to sanctify by prayer the dead moments in our daily life when we seem to have nothing to do, when we must wait in queue. The small annoyances and joys of the day can become reminders to us of God and of prayer. All these things can be learned and practiced.

Happiness through Prayer, 51

One can live to the glory of God implicitly, silently, in a general, diffuse intention that nevertheless impregnates everything. It is not just our head, our little thoughts, that must think of God but also our activities, our life, all our being. And where the heart is alive, experiencing the griefs and the joys of life as they really are, where the heart has not culpably shut itself away from this authentic existence, there the heart does think of God though without so much as one explicit word.

Biblical Homilies, 153

God, give us the inner strength and steadfastness to keep our hearts awake, ready to say yes without reserve when the time comes to say it, despite all our worldly wisdom, all our contrivances, all our compromises, so that by your grace our poor divided lives may receive that perfection which can be ours for eternity.

Biblical Homilies, 120

Prayer in everyday life is difficult. It is easily forgotten, since our rushed and fevered age does not foster and promote it. It is even more difficult to make everyday prayer *real* prayer and to prevent its degenerating into mere routine. We must ask ourselves how far our everyday prayer is more than mere words. Heart and mind are often far away from what we are saying. Instead of speaking heart to heart to God, we recite set formulas. Our main concern is to get through the formulas, and there is no attempt to establish vital contact with God.

Thus everyday prayer becomes an everyday matter in the worst sense of the word. It becomes superficial, mechanical, slipshod lip service, the performance of an external task to be got through as quickly as possible in order to get back to more pleasant things.

Thus we slip into that terrifying state of everyday Christian life where in praying our hearts remain far from God. Our lips honor God, but our heart does not join with them; and yet we imagine that we thus fulfill our duty toward God.

In many cases, we suffer because of the difference between what our prayer is and what we know it should be. We suffer from our heart's refusing to enter into the lofty words of adoration, praise, thanks, petition, awe, or contrition, which are the subject and expression of prayer. We suffer from the contrast between our willingness to pray, often and everyday, and our apparent incapability. Our heart seems to be paralyzed, and we fear that we may be labeled a hypocrite through pretending to do something that in reality is beyond our power. We think that in sincerity toward ourself and toward God we must wait until the fountains in the depths of our heart spring up again, to provide the healing waters of grace, of spontaneous emotion and of vital spiritual experience, thus making true prayer possible in a sincere outpouring of the heart.

Nevertheless, in spite of all these difficulties, it remains true, as the wisdom of our forefathers and our own precious inheritance teach us, that we must make prayer part of our daily life. We must not restrict prayer to the rare moments of sensible devotion when prayer wells up spontaneously within us.

Happiness through Prayer, 46, 47

L ord accept my poor heart. It is often so far from you. It is like a wasteland without water, lost in the innumerable things and trifles that fill my everyday life. Only you, Lord, can focus my heart on you, who are the center of all hearts and the Lord of every soul. Only you can give the spirit of prayer, only your grace is capable of granting me the ability to find you through the multiplicity of things and the distraction of mind of everyday routine, you the one thing necessary, the one thing in which my heart can rest. May your Spirit come to the help of my weakness, and when we do not know what we should ask, may he intercede for us with inexpressible sighs, and you who know men's hearts will hear what your Spirit interceding for us desires in us.

Everyday Faith, 209

When we pray, are we only little beggars before God, wrapped up in our own worries? Is our heart ever enlarged in thanksgiving—as it were a great preface in the Eucharist of which our life is the celebration—thanksgiving that we Christians are created, called, sanctified, redeemed, pardoned, preserved, rescued in God's providence, that we are God's beloved children, that God's Spirit is given to us, that eternal life awaits us, that the Lord is nigh, that he is kind and clement, and that his mercy is unbounded?

Do we ever give thanks that our thanksgiving and our petitions reach the ears of God, and that we ask God to perfect the good work that he has begun in us on the day of Christ that is not far off?

Biblical Homilies, 140

Heaven and earth are realities. On the one hand, there is the living, free, and almighty God; on the other, there is the truly free nature of the human person, his creature. These two freedoms meet in prayer, wherein we find a cry of distress, a pleading for some good, coexisting with an attitude of complete submission to the inscrutable judgments of God. These two aspects—our freedom to plead, our submission to the free decision of God—are always found together in true prayer. "Unless you become as little children," said Christ, thereby pointing to the sublime virtue of simplicity which is the essence of Christian perfection. To lead a truly Christian life is to place one's whole being into the hands of God as confidently as a child takes the guiding hand of its father. The child's confidence is complete and without the slightest trace of reservation. The hand it grasps is of one who knows best, who loves, who will not lead it into any danger, who will shelter it from evil—but who certainly will not reach down that sharp knife or that poisonous liquid, however much the child, fascinated by the glitter or the color, may clamor to have it. The profoundest secret of the Christian life and of Christian prayer is to become a child in our relations with God, a child whose quiet confidence and silent submission do not fail in moments of trial when God appears to have turned from us.

Happiness through Prayer, 67

Our Father who are in the depths of my heart, transforming its hollow emptiness into a heaven on earth;

Hallowed be thy Name, even in the deathlike silence of my ignorance and my lack of faith;

Thy kingdom come in the very midst of my desolation;

Thy will be done in me, even if it means pain and death;

Thy will be done in me, for thy will is my true life;

Give us this day our daily bread, for I am utterly dependent upon thy divine providence;

Forgive us our trespasses—those sins that are ultimately but treason against thy love for us, and therefore treason against myself;

Deliver us from evil—from the evil of centering our lives upon ourselves, in order that we may learn that thou art the center of all, and that only in thee can we find freedom worthy of the children of God.

Happiness through Prayer, 19

7

OUR FAITH KNOWS THAT FAITH MEANS FAITH WITHIN THE CHURCH

I believe in the eternity of God who has entered into our time, my time. Beneath the wearisome coming and going of time, life that no longer knows death is already secretly growing. It is already there, it is already in me precisely because I believe. For the cycle of birth and death to stand still in the true reality, all I have to do is believe in the coming of God into our time, really believe. In the act of believing, I patiently bear with time, with its hard and bitter demand that brings death in its wake. And I dwell no longer on the thought that time has the last word to say, which is a denial.

The Eternal Year, 17

We too should be the voice of one crying in the wilderness, should cry to God continually, although our cry seems to be swallowed up by endless silence and solitude, and even when there seems to be no answer to our call. We shall hear the answer. It is not just an echo, not simply consolation in the faith; it is the eternal Word of God himself, filling this emptiness, the wilderness of my heart that is so often left waiting without hope and without faith, in the desolation of this life—filling it with eternal light, eternal truth, the eternal reality that is the only reality.

Biblical Homilies, 66–7

For us Jesus is God's answer to the one comprehensive question that we ourselves are and that we are posed. In belief in him as God's ultimate definitive answer to us, we are confident that the mystery we call God will, in forgiveness and final blessedness, communicate himself to us in that which we call the Holy Spirit of God and, in that Spirit's definitive overshadowing of us, eternal life.

We believe in Jesus the Christ, that is, in God's self-promise in forgiveness and eternal life which has been persuasively announced in his life. No one forces us to accept in faith God's answer, who is Jesus crucified and risen. But also no one can convince us that there is another, better, and more comprehensive answer to the question ineluctably and inexorably posed by our own life, even when we try to ignore this question. No one will persuade us that we have not heard the question. Once we pose it and face up to it, we find it easy to believe that in Jesus we have heard an answer to it.

This answer does not answer all the thousand and one questions of a particular kind that our life poses, but it contains all these individual answered or unanswered questions in the saving mystery of God. All these questions of life ultimately come together in the one question that death poses in our life. But we have the courage of believing hope to fall with Jesus' death into the abyss of God as into our own definitiveness, our home, and our eternal life.

Christian at the Crossroads, 34–5

A faith that is honest about its subjective insecurity is more secure than one that basks in an enforced, self-satisfied, subjective security. This impartial assessment of

70

faith could and ought also to be allowed expression in public attitudes in the Church. A faith aware of its subjective vulnerability cannot be assimilated to that deliberate doubt in matters of faith that moralists discuss and characterize as sin.

Opportunities for Faith, 56

O ur conception of the Christian faith is often too one-sided. We conceive it only as a set list of determined facts that must be held as true. These facts stand by themselves on this list, and we just think about them. These facts, however, are fundamentally an event that still endures. We are situated in the midst of this event, and we are, precisely through faith, drawn into it, so that we are caught up in it.

By means of faith the salvation of the believer really takes place in the believer himself. Salvation itself comes out from the past into his present, into him, and it becomes present in his time. Christ lives in him. The believer becomes subject to the inner law of each event that is believed. In a mysterious way he becomes a contemporary of the incarnate Son of God. He dies and lives with him. The reason is that through faith Christ lives, in the Holy Spirit, in the believer. Furthermore, in all truth and all reality, this Spirit is gradually shaping the life of the believer into the image of the life and destiny of the incarnate Word of the Father.

Moreover, by this very fact, Christ is in a mysterious way already present in the believer as his future. This future has already come into the believer in a hidden way; he is already, in a hidden way, what he will be when all that is now hidden is un-

71

veiled. What will one day be our complete perfection has already begun. And this reality begins percisely because we believe.

The Eternal Year, 14, 15

Where a person lives her life in unconditional selfless love, in an ultimate loyalty that goes unrewarded, in responsible acceptance of the dictates of autarchic conscience—solitary and unsung as it is—she is living out a hoping belief in her permanent definitiveness, whether she reflects about it, manages to objectify this conviction verbally or not.

Whoever stands before the graves of Auschwitz or Bangladesh or other monuments to the absurdity of human life, and manages neither to run away (because she cannot tolerate this absurdity) nor to fall into cynical doubt, believes in what we Christians call eternal life, even though her mind does not grasp it.

Christian at the Crossroads, 88

Our faith, this bitter, burdensome yet tenacious faith, without false pathos or the front of pose, is just one constant "Lord help my unbelief." Our faith is upheld by the last ounce of strength in our heart and is at the same time the ultimate strength for our heart. Therefore, faith is not curious. In calling out to God it finds him on the cross of Christ whom we tormented unto death; faith reaches for the sacrament, because it wants to meet the word of grace just where we are, on this earth and in this finite hour; it knows that faith means faith within the Church.

What the Church speaks is our light and our strength: the Love of the living God even in darkness; the word of reconciliation in spite of the experience of our sin; the word of the Holy Spirit poured out into our hearts in the face of our being tired, faint, and empty. In short, the word of Jesus Christ, Son of God and truly man, crucified, raised into the eternal life of God, explorer of human fate, presence of God in the world, source of salvation and of peace, Lord of all who believe in him and entrust their fate to his shelter, head of all who are called and saved, who with him form the one community of love and mercy that we call the Church: visible like he himself in the ministers of the Church, in the written and proclaimed Word, and in the visible sacrament.

Vom Glauben inmitten der Welt, 28
Translated by Renate Craine

W e are the believers in God and Jesus Christ in brotherly and sisterly communion, and consequently we are the Church. We experience this faith as our redeemed freedom and as a mission to the world, which by means of this faith throughout its entire history is to find God as its definitive goal. Naturally this community of belief, called the Church, elaborates its social structures, its officials, its changing history all too often laden with human narrowness, guilt, and disunion, on the pattern of the needs of human association, according to God's and Jesus' will. We who really know, however, what this community of belief is ultimately concerned with, namely God in Jesus Christ, can endure this believing communion with calm patience—even though it is composed of poor human beings who, also as Church, are on their way from guilt to forgiveness—knowing as we do that we contribute our own narrowness and guilt to this community that is centered on and borne up by Christ.

At its deepest level our Christian faith is simple, living, inexhaustible, and, because it concerns our ultimate destiny, valid and effective for today and for tomorrow. We can still confidently believe today if our spirit and our heart have really found this inmost center of the Christian faith. We may still notice that many individual developments of this simple faith in the almost incalculable mass of individual doctrines remain alien and well-nigh unintelligible. We can, however, confidently and humbly let them rest, trusting that our own understanding of the faith will grow and mature into a closer and closer assimilation to the belief of the Church in all times and cultures. We can still believe as Christians and Catholics today, even though we know that our own faith is still on the way and as long as we do not turn our momentary understanding into the definitive norm of faith.

Christian at the Crossroads, 36

In the Church and in the Body of Christ each has his or her own particular function and mission. We must all be Christians and nothing else, but this is the very reason why each of us must accomplish *our* mission in *self*-effacement and simply must not behave as if everything that is realized of Christianity in the world and in the Church has also to come about with the same intensity, clarity, and vitality in our own lives.

Each of us does what God has assigned to him and leaves the other person to go her own way; he does not feel that the other —with her mission, with her vocation, with her perhaps very secular life—threatens or denies the value of his own life; nor does the other person feel threatened in her own turn.

Opportunities for Faith, 72, 73

It goes without saying that every true Christian laments the social and historical shape of the Church, which in its tangible reality is bound to lag behind its essence. The Church proclaims a message that always calls its empirical reality into question. It is always the Church of sinners, whose members belie with their deeds what they confess with their lips. Frightful and mean things have blotted its history, so much so that only one consideration keep us in it: where else could we go if we left the Church? Would we be true to the liberating Spirit of Jesus if we, who are ourselves selfish sinners, claimed to be the "pure" by keeping this poor Church at a distance?

The sole hope of doing one's bit to remedy the Church's wretchedness lies in bearing the burden of its misery, of which each member is to some extent guilty; in trying to live *in* the Church as a Christian, in bearing the responsibility for transforming it again and again from within (in all its denominations, it must always be the Church of the "Reformation").

Christian at the Crossroads, 28

We know from our faith that God's grace is not confined to the visible Church of Christ, that God's grace comes and goes through all the alleyways of the world and finds everywhere hearts in which supernatural salvation is wrought through this faith and this grace. So we Catholics should not fall into the mistake of thinking that, because we are the children of the true Church, there can be no divine grace or love except in our hearts. We must be told again and again what the Gospel tells us, that the children of the kingdom can be among those cast out, while others who did not seem to be chosen will come from the four corners of the earth and be numbered among the elect.

So let us follow the example of the Lord and be open and generous in recognizing whatever is good, whatever is noble and active and admirable and alive, wherever it may be, in recognizing that grace can also work outside the visible Church.

Biblical Homilies, 20–1

The individual parish, while standing in legitimate unity with the whole Church, is itself Church and not just an administrative branch of the great Church that ministers to the religious needs and individual salvation of people through the local establishment. A parish is local Church. What the Church exists for has to happen there: the experience of the Holy Spirit in freedom and love, a witness of eternal hope to the world at large, an active love of such unconditional nature as is only possible when people meet in the freeing love of God, the celebration of Jesus' Last Supper in which his death and resurrection become present as the historical, tangible testimony that God in his glory gives himself to us as our salvation. Everything else in the Church—pope and bishops, clergy and authority, organization and everything else—are only means to that one end that should become embodied in the parish and visible in the world: God and our life in him in freedom, forgiveness, and love. Parish is Church.

All of us are Church. All of us are not only those who are ministered to by an official Church but also those who are Church, compelled to shape, mold, and live Church, that Church that is the magnificent community of all with Jesus in his Spirit. From this follows that the Christian should not make demands upon the Church as an organization that is external to himself, but that he has to be aware of his blessed and responsible task, that he together with others must become Church. Criticism of the Church is permitted and necessary. But everyone who criticizes the Church must always start by asking one crucial question: Have I fulfilled my responsibility to be Church with others in love, cooperation, tolerance, patience, and in the knowledge that I can never fully satisfy my own responsibility for the Church.

Herausforderung des Christen, 64
Translated by Renate Craine

A thousand things in the Church do not suit us. This is perfectly plain. But why should they have to suit us? If the Church had to be just precisely the way we would like it, what would everyone else do? Are we not, all unawares, objectively risking a shameless individualism and selfishness when we seek to live in the Church in such a way as baldly to arrange it to our own taste? When we feel, perhaps with some justification, that a bishop fails to "suit" us, do we still treat him as a brother with whom we live in community for better or for worse?

Difficult as it may be for us, we live today in a concrete world Church, with its historical conditions and with the limitations and tentative character of the phase through which it happens to be going at the moment. Of course it has not yet reached a later, better phase. But it is in this Church that we must live.

The Love of Jesus and the Love of Neighbor, 86

Not everyone who says, "Lord, Lord," enters the kingdom of heaven. The Catholic whose practice is really sufficient for the kingdom of heaven has to practice not only in Church but also in life, and has in fact to practice patience, an unassuming spirit, love of neighbor, honesty, and all those virtues in which the children of the world often seem to be superior to us. Orthodoxy and the faith that truly justifies are two different things. Someone with "a clean slate" may have a heart that lacks God and real love. Churchgoing is not in itself true Christianity. In fact orthodoxy, respectability, and fidelity to the Church can present the danger of self-righteousness and pious hypocrisy.

We ought to keep a lookout for the "Christian pagans," that is, people who are near to God without realizing it, but from whom the light is hidden by the shadow that we throw. From

East and West people are entering the kingdom of God by roads that are not shown on any official map. When we meet them they ought to be able to see from us that the official paths on which we are traveling are safer and shorter.

Everyday Faith, 128, 129

The prayer to the Holy Spirit means a readiness to admit into life the incalculable, the new that becomes old, the old becoming new; it often means having no clearly worked-out answer in the concrete situation, but continuing, because the past provides enough reason for hope, but in fact only for hope.

The word of the Holy Spirit does not provide prescriptions that we merely need to carry out. It commands boldness, experiment, decision, which cannot be justified by general principles (the law and the letter). The word of the Holy Spirit is the question to each individual in his or her irreplaceable uniqueness as to whether he or she has the courage to venture, to experiment, to endure the opposition of the great mass— whether he or she trusts in the Holy Spirit. With this courage everyone in the Church must do her own part, even though at first sight she is not in agreement with what others do. Each must do this conscious of the fact that her gift and her mission are different from the Spirit's gift to others. But if the unity of the Spirit in the variety of his gifts is to be maintained, there are in fact *many* gifts. This unity exists for us only if we blast open what the Spirit has given us for our own—so that we do this and not something else—in the loving hope that all these gifts are one, even though we cannot see into and control this unity.

Opportunities for Faith, 44–5

8

I KNEEL BEFORE YOUR
BLESSED CROSS

If I do not know myself and my origin, if my destiny is hidden from me, if I stand in fear before myself and before the chasms of my heart—where should I stay, if not before the cross, in which the incomprehensibility of human destiny becomes the revelation that God is truly love. I kneel before him. And I am silent.

For what shall I tell him, except what I am? And if I have never understood myself, what else can I do except surrender myself to him completely, to him whose love, loyal even to death, alone has understood me? And if this ego silently loves and lovingly commits itself, then it perceives that it finds its true essence and its genuine likeness precisely in the crucified.

The Eternal Year, 84

We all are gathered round the cross of the Crucified, whether we look up to him or try to look past him, whether we are at the moment quite cheerful and happy (this is not forbidden) or frightened to death. We are standing under the cross, being ourselves delivered to death, imprisoned in guilt, disappointed, deficient in love, selfish and cowardly, suffering through ourselves, through others, through life itself, which we do not understand. Of course, if we are just quite comfortable we protest against such a pessimistic outlook that wants to take away our joy in life (which is quite untrue); when we are vigorous in body and soul we refuse to believe that this will not last forever. Yet we are always under the cross.

Would it not therefore be a good thing to look up to him whom they have pierced, as scripture expresses it? Ought we not to admit what we have suppressed and to want to stand where we actually do stand? Surely we ought to have the courage to let our heart be seized by God's grace and to accept the scandal and absurdity of our inescapable situation as "the power of God and the wisdom of God" by looking up at the Crucified and entering into the mystery of his death.

Many certainly do this without being aware of it by their way of life that accepts death in silent obedience. But we may also fail to do this. Hence it is better expressly to celebrate the Good Friday of the Lord by approaching his cross and speaking his last words with him. They are quite simple; everyone can understand and say them with him. This is the abyss of existence into which we fall. And we believe that there dwell love and life themselves. We say Father, into your hands I commend myself, my spirit, my life, and my death. We have done all we could do—the other, the ineffable that is salvation, will come too.

Grace in Freedom, 123–4

What do we mean when we speak of the cross, of the passion, of death in relation to Jesus? In him these words had certainly a very deep and mysterious meaning. Nevertheless, the Son of Man, too, experienced them as we do, only today we use different expressions. What is meant by them does not take place only in those moments when the incomprehensibility of life can no longer be shirked, for example, when our dearest die, when a lifelong love is forever destroyed by unfaithfulness, when the doctor tells us that death is imminent and inevitable. What is meant is always present, especially if we do not want to admit it, if we suppress it and cover it over. It is always there: in the mute presence of death throughout our life, in the loneliness that is there even when we are quite near to our beloved, in the colorless daily round, in the thankless performance of our duty selfishly exploited by others, in the fatigue and deterioration of our life, which was once so marvelously colorful and exuberant. This passion and death are present when the inner voice through which a person had expressed him or herself has ceased to make itself heard and when all our life and all our hopes have ended in inevitable disappointment.

We ought to allow our living experience once more to fill the empty verbal shells of an all-too-familiar religious language, so that the word of the cross and of the imitation of the crucified Lord might suddenly receive an intelligible content and a power that force us to make a decision. Then we would know that we must truly act out our faith when we are asked: Do you accept the cross of your life, do you know that it means sharing in the passion of the Lord? Then we would meet not only in the liturgy of the Church but in our very life the words: Hail, cross, our only hope in Passiontide, the passion that is also ever present and is always suffered even in the most commonplace life.

Grace in Freedom, 119

We participate in the passion of Christ not so much by indulging in pious feelings, but by bearing the burdens of our life with simple fortitude and without ostentation. For we share by faith in the passion of our Lord precisely by realizing that our life is a participation in his destiny. We find this difficult, because so often we fail to understand that the bitterness and burden of our own life do—or should—give us a mysterious share in the destiny of all men. Internal and external distress carries the deadly danger of egoism, because it tempts us to think only of ourselves, to be concerned only with our own affairs and thus to increase our distress by our self-centered loneliness in a vicious circle.

But it should and it can be different. We can freely accept our own distress as our contribution to the destiny of all men, whose burdens are thus mysteriously lightened. This can be verified in everyday life. The person who suffers selfishly, who rebels and complains, actually seeks to transfer his or her own burden to others, instead of bearing it silently so that it may be easier for them. But this is only the commonplace appearance of a more profound, all-pervading law: We always also bear the burden in a thousand different ways that we do not know at all, beyond the restrictions of time and space to the very limits of human history.

If we were aware of this, we would also better understand that we can share in the passion of the Son of Man, we would understand that his passion is the unique acceptance of the passion of mankind, in which it is accepted, suffered, redeemed, and freed into the mystery of God.

Grace in Freedom, 117–8

O Lord, when shall I once and for all grasp this, this law of your life and so of my life? The law that death is life, losing oneself is finding oneself, poverty is riches, and suffering is a grace, that to reach the end in truth is fulfillment.

Watch and Pray with Me, 57–8

The incomprehensibility of suffering is part of the incomprehensibility of God, not in the sense that we can deduce the incomprehensibility as necessary and yet see this necessity enlightened by something else we know about God. That would not be incomprehensibility. Suffering, as something real and forever incomprehensible, is a real manifestation of the incomprehensibility of God in his being and in his freedom. In his being, because in spite of the dread and (we could say) amorality of suffering (that of children and innocents at least), we have to confess the pure goodness of God that has no need to be acquitted by our court of justice. In his freedom, especially when ordaining the suffering of creatures, there is incomprehensibility, precisely because the holy purpose of this freedom that ordains suffering could be fulfilled without suffering. Suffering in itself is the irreducible manifestation of the incomprehensibility of God.

The acceptance of suffering without an answer that would differ from the incomprehensibility of God and his freedom is the concrete way in human existence in which we accept God himself and let him be God. There is no blissful light to illuminate the unfathomable darkness of suffering but God himself. One finds God only in the loving acceptance of just this incomprehensibility, without which he would not be God.

Worte vom Kreuz, 39, 43
Translated by Renate Craine

Where do we find the strength, in the darkness of suffering and in the powerlessness this effects in us, to really give the answer that is demanded of us, an answer that appears to be arduous beyond words although it seems merely to entail the silent, willing acceptance of suffering and of its incomprehensibility? And where do we find the ultimate confidence that our yes to the incomprehensibility of God will once more be accepted as the answer given by God with God himself to the last word of a human being?

As Christians we believe in faith that the answer demanded of us in our suffering is only possible in a grace-given "co-consumation" of the answer Jesus gave on the cross to his death agony when he allowed himself to become engulfed by it: "Father, into your hands I commend my spirit." The Christian is convinced in faith that the Resurrected One is the One who was crucified and died and vice versa, and that therefore the question of whether complete surrender to the mystery of God and of death is truly accepted by God as eternally valid and eternally sanctifying has been answered by God with God himself.

Worte vom Kreuz, 44–5
Translated by Renate Craine

Cross and resurrection go together in every authentic belief in Jesus. The cross means the demand, never more to be veiled, for our unconditional surrender to the mystery of existence that we can no longer bring under our control because we are finite and guilt-laden. Resurrection means the unconditioned hope that in that surrender we are definitively accepted by this mystery in forgiveness and blessedness, that where we let go completely, the precipice disappears. The cross and resurrection of Jesus mean that this letting-go and not-falling because of God's activity have become, in Jesus, exemplary, and that this possibility (and also the possibility of being able to let go, which is the most difficult challenge of our lives) is irrevocably promised to us too.

Here, in Jesus, we have the actual absolute. We need only commit ourselves, lovingly and unconditionally, to this real person. Then we have everything. It is true that we must die with him. But then nobody escapes dying. Why not with him, as one with him, we say: "My God, why have you deserted me?" and "Into your hands I commit my spirit"?

Not in speaking about death, but in death, his and one's own. In that moment, which for each individual is still to come, we have laid hold of Christianity.

We may, however, prepare ourselves here and now to be open to that event. The glory of life does not vanish in it. On the contrary, everything receives its ultimate weight for the first time and yet becomes the "light burden." It is grace, but grace offered to all, which can still be accepted and (as our Christian hope affirms) is still accepted even where the unconditional hope has not yet explicitly found the one it seeks as its realization: Jesus of Nazareth. Perhaps it is decreed that many "find" him more easily when they seek him only in nameless hope, without being able to call him by his historical name. However, the person who has sufficiently and clearly encountered him must confess him, because otherwise he or she would be denying his or her own hope.

Christian at the Crossroads, 25–6

Hope condenses the experience of life into two words: mystery and death. "Mystery" expresses this helplessness in hope. "Death," however, commands us not to veil this helplessness but to endure it. I look on Jesus the crucified and know that nothing will be spared me. I give myself (I hope) into his death, and hope that that joint death is the ascent of the blessed mystery. In this hope, however, life in all its beauty emerges in the darkness and everything becomes promise. I find that being a Christian is the simplest possible task, the utterly simple, and therefore so difficult, light burden, as the Gospel calls it. If we bear it, it bears us. The longer we live, the more difficult and the lighter it becomes.

Christian at the Crossroads, 30

Jesus' death has filled the ordinary death we all have in common and share with him with blessed hope. That which nobody is spared, which makes everything provisional and questionable, which seems to make everything equal and indifferent in that same decline, has itself become the sign of limitless, endless hope and gives everything else its final dignity and meaning. Everything that with its own spirit, glory, and blessedness seemed only to reach the close frontier of death that negates all now bears an unending glory and promise that truly is no longer limited by death.

If all of our days seem ordinary because of the relentlessness with which they lead to death that equalizes all, these days

have become, for anyone who in faith truly understands Jesus'
death, days of celebration where the event of an eternal life
happens and where everything commonplace is gifted with
eternal dignity.

Herausforderung des Christen, 42
Translated by Renate Craine

The believing, hoping consent manifested in Jesus' death to
the incomprehensibility of death in which God dwells is
demanded of us as well in our death. Just as we have to let go
and surrender ourselves in death without letting this need for
self-surrender turn into sheer despair, so we can only consum-
mate this self-surrender through God's deed for us in his Spirit,
who even in the death of Jesus made possible and carried out
this self-surrender through Jesus' acceptance. In this he promised us that this miracle of the transformation of despair into
the self-surrendering acceptance of the incomprehensibility
that we call God would be effective in our death as well. We
cannot simply *know* that this miracle of hoping self-surrender
which hopes against all hope takes place also in us, but we can
hope for it unflinchingly.

For this abides: The redeeming self-surrender of Jesus
spreads to us if we are willing. We die with him and in him.
This self-surrender must, of course, be practiced in the ordinariness of life, in the inevitable but calmly accepted renuncia-
tions of everyday life with its banality and aridity, with its hid-

den bitterness for which we receive no thanks. If we practice "dying with Jesus" in this way, if we walk toward the hoped-for miracle that in our death willing self-surrender comes to pass through the Spirit of God who grants the acceptance of God, then our life in its sober ordinariness becomes sheer gratitude for the cross.

The blessed hope of the Christian is that God himself will support us with his strength in the abyss of our helplessness in death, so that not only will life follow after death, but this death itself, through the power of God, becomes our own deed that creates life, so that the willing self-surrender becomes the deed that creates eternity.

Death, which is our real cross and also the participation in the cross of Christ, is really not just an event at the end of our life but involves dying throughout all of life. All our experiences of finitude, all bitterness and disappointments, the decline of our strength, experiences of being unsuccessful, of emptiness and aridity, of pain, misery, and need, of force and injustice are just forerunners, yes, parts of the one death we die throughout our lives. It is because of this that the willing, hoping, self-surrendering acceptance of the thousandfold experiences of death in life are just as much part of that gratitude for the cross we suffer and enter into if we calmly die. Gratitude for the cross can thus become a blessed ordinary thing. It does not consist of melancholy ideologies; it does not happen through powerful words and sublime feelings. True gratitude for the cross is rather that simple, calm acceptance of a slow dying, happening throughout all of life, that represses nothing through utopian ideologies.

Herausforderung des Christen, 44, 46
Translated by Renate Craine

Our death is the hour of decision. The whole of a human life is gathered into that hour, and our past appears clear, solid, and final at that moment when time for us is to be swallowed up in eternity. In the hour of death, both God and the dying person speak their last word—a word that is final and decisive for all eternity.

The important question for us is whether we shall obtain the grace to make our last conscious moment a moment filled with the prayer of decision, by which we mean such a prayer as will lift up all that we were and are, all that we have done and suffered, in oblation to the mercy of God; whether, as the shades of death darken in our minds, we shall turn a last glance of faith on him who has crossed the bar of death and yet, behold, he lives. Shall we say to him at that moment: "Come, Lord Jesus"? Shall we be able to pray in that hour of decision, to commend our souls into the hands of God? May God mercifully grant us the grace to depart from this world in prayer, so that the last thought in our minds may fit us for life everlasting. Blessed is the person who can utter a prayer of decision when the hour comes that is the most decisive of all.

We do not know whether we shall be given the grace to meet death with full consciousness, greeting it with prayer and resignation as the messenger of God. For death comes like a thief in the night.

That prayer of decision that we wish to say in the hour of our death must be said by us again and again during our life. We must pray now for the decision of that future hour, and we must pray for the grace of fortitude. Let us pray that God may prevent us from being separated from him, and that even when we are about to leave him, he will not leave us, but lovingly compel our wayward heart back into his service, through his almighty and mysteriously gentle grace.

Happiness through Prayer, 107–8

SOURCES

Biblical Homilies. Translated by Desmond Forristal and Richard Strachan. © 1966 Herder KG. Original edition. *Biblische Predigten.* Herder, Freiburg im Breisgau, 1965.

Christian at the Crossroads. Translated by V. Green. English translation © Search Press Limited, 1975. Original edition: *Wagnis des Christen.* © Verlag Herder KG, Freiburg im Breisgau.

Encounters with Silence. Translated by James M. Demske, S.J. © 1960 by the Newman Press. Original edition: *Worte ins Schweigen.* Innsbruck, 1938.

The Eternal Year. Translated by John Shea, S.S. Copyright © 1964 Helicon Press, Inc. Original edition: *Kleines Kirchenjahr.* Verlag Ars Sacra Joseph Müller, Munich, 1953.

Everyday Faith. Translated by W. J. O'Hara. © 1967 Herder KG. Original edition: *Glaube, der die Erde liebt.* Herder, Freiburg im Breisgau, 1966.

"Experiencing the Spirit," translated by John Griffiths and copyright © Herder KG 1979, was published in *The Spirit in the Church* (London: Search Press, New York: The Seabury Press, 1979). Original edition: *Erfahrung des Geistes.* Copyright © Verlag Herder, Freiburg im Breisgau, 1977.

Grace in Freedom. Translated and adapted by Hilda Graef. © 1969 Herder KG. Original edition: *Gnade als Freiheit*. Herder, Freiburg im Breisgau, 1968.

Happiness through Prayer. Translator not given. Copyright by Clonmore & Reynolds, Ltd., Dublin. First published 1958. Original edition: *Von der Not und dem Segen des Gebets*. Innsbruck, 1949.

Herausforderung des Christen: Meditationen, Reflexionen, Interviews. Herder, Freiburg im Breisgau, 1975.

The Love of Jesus and the Love of Neighbor. Translated by Robert Barr. English translation copyright © 1983. Original editions: *Was heisst Jesus lieben?* © Verlag Herder, Freiburg im Breisgau, 1982 and *Wer ist dein Bruder?* © Verlag Herder, Freiburg im Breisgau, 1981.

Mary Mother of the Lord. Translated by W. J. O'Hara. © 1963 Herder KG. Original edition: *Maria, Mutter des Herrn*. Herder, Freiburg im Breisgau.

Meditations on Hope and Love. Translated by V. Green. © 1976 Search Press Limited. Original editions: *Was sollen wir jetzt tun?* and *Gott ist Mensch geworden*. © 1974, 1975 Verlag Herder KG, Freiburg im Breisgau.

Opportunities for Faith: Elements of a Modern Spirituality. Translated by Edward Quinn. English translation copyright © 1974 by S.P.C.K. Original edition: *Chancen des Glaubens*. Copyright © 1970 by Verlag Herder KG, Freiburg im Breisgau.

Über die Geduld (with Eberhard Jüngel). Herder, Freiburg im Breisgau, 1983.

Watch and Pray with Me. Translated by William V. Dych, S.J. © 1966 by Herder and Herder, Incorporated. Original edition: *Heilige Stunde und Passionsandacht*. Innsbruck, 1949 (under pseudonym Anselm Trescher)

Worte vom Kreuz. Herder, Freiburg im Breisgau, 1980.